MW00782093

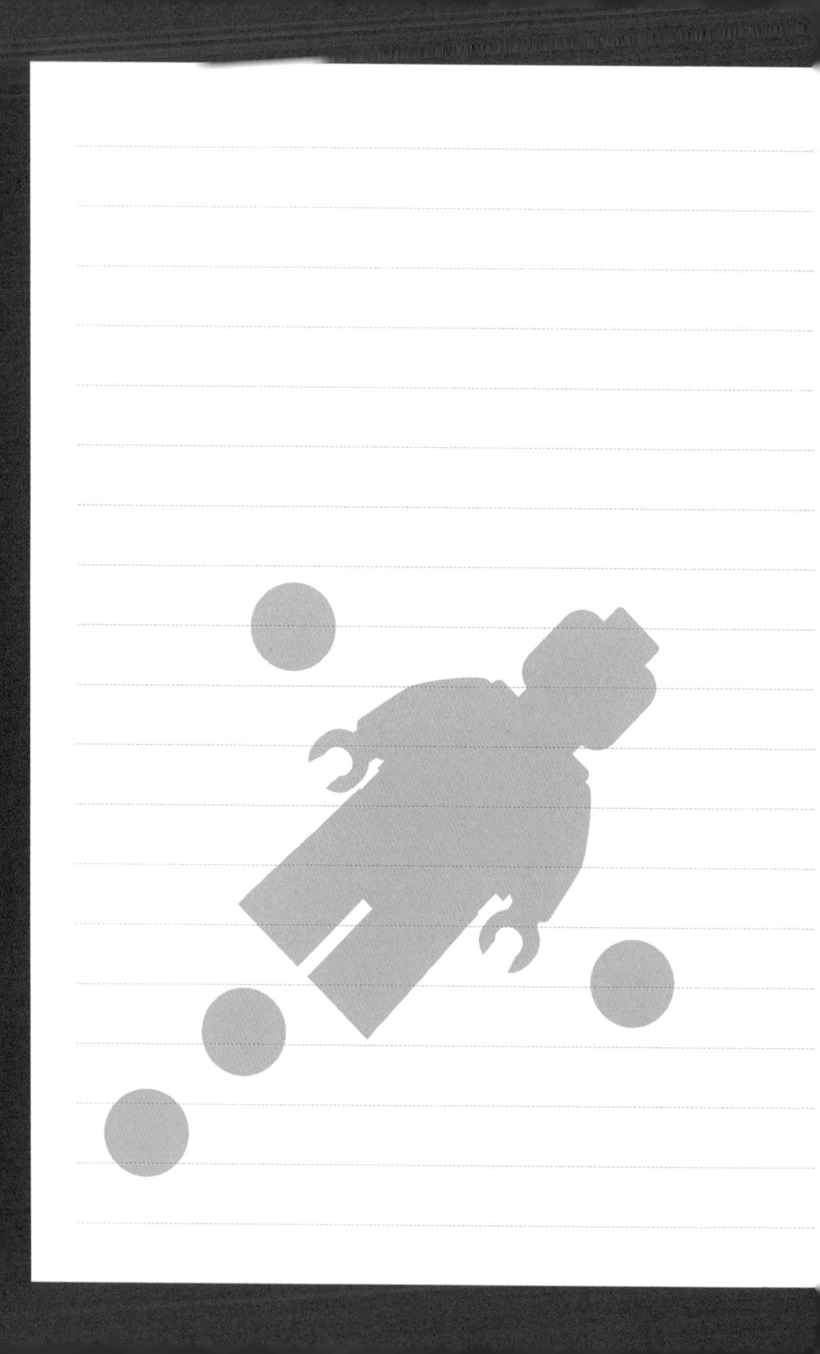

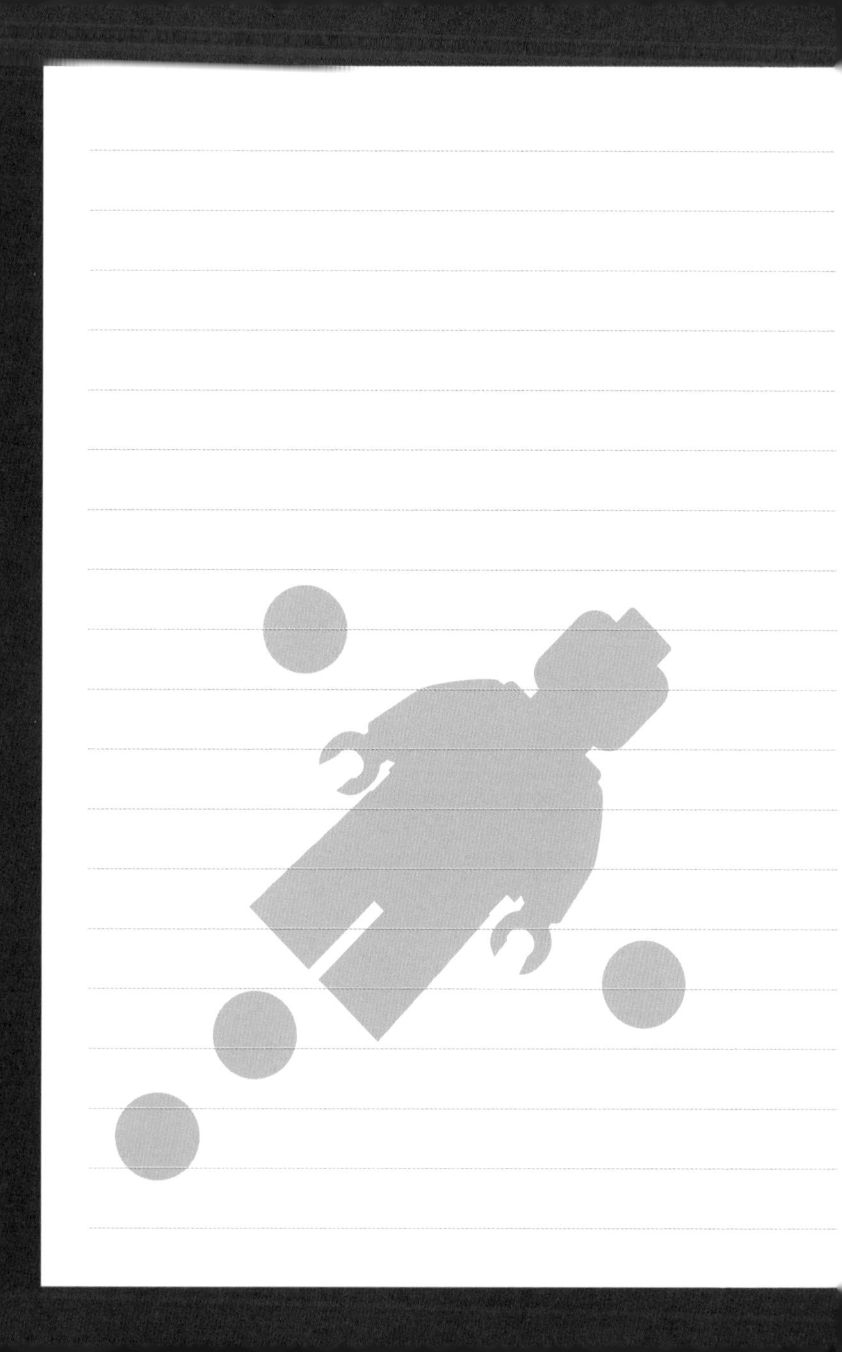

LEGO, the LEGO logo, the Minifigure, and the Brick and Knob configurations are trademarks and/or copyrights of the LEGO Group. ©2020 The LEGO Group. All rights reserved. Manufactured by Chronicle Books, 680 Second Street, San Francisco, CA 94107 under license from the LEGO Group. Made in China by C&C Joint Printing Co., Shanghai, China, July 2020.

Copyright ©2020 Warner Bros. Entertainment Inc. & The LEGO Group. THE LEGO® MOVIE 2 © & ™ Warner Bros. Entertainment Inc., & The LEGO Group. LEGO, the LEGO logo, the Minifigure, and the Brick and Knob configurations are trademarks and/or copyrights of the LEGO Group. ©2020 The LEGO Group. All Rights Reserved. WB SHIELD: ™ & © WBEI. (s20)

ISBN 978-1-4521-8199-8

Artwork by Blake Powell.
Design by Sara Schneider.

See the full range of LEGO® books and gift products at www.chroniclebooks.com.

10 9 8 7 6 5 4 3 2 1

CHRONICLE BOOKS
680 SECOND STREET
SAN FRANCISCO, CA 94107